Contents

5·99

GRADE ONE SCALES
MADE FUN BY

MALCOLM ARCHER

Kevin
Mayhew

We hope you enjoy *Snakes and Ladders*.
Further copies of this and other enjoyable collections are available from your local music shop.

In case of difficulty, please contact the publisher direct:

The Sales Department
KEVIN MAYHEW LTD
Rattlesden
Bury St Edmunds
Suffolk IP30 0SZ

Phone 01449 737978
Fax 01449 737834

Please ask for our complete catalogue of outstanding Instrumental Music.

Front cover illustration by Sara Silcock
Cover designed by Veronica Ward and Graham Johstone

First published in Great Britain in 1995 by Kevin Mayhew Ltd

ISBN 0 86209 743 6
Catalogue No: 3611179

Music Editor: Rosalind Dean and Tamzin Howard
Music Setting: Rosalind Dean

Printed and bound in Great Britain
by Caligraving Limited Thetford Norfolk

Dear Budding Pianist,

Scales and arpeggios are fun! The pieces in *Snakes and Ladders* will help you learn your scales and arpeggios in an interesting way.

In this book you can slide *Up and Down a Rainbow*, take *A Walk in the Wood*, jive with *Jazzy Fingers* and feast on a *Moonlight Breakfast*. Or how about waltzing on Wednesday, a jeté on a banana skin and a walk with a three legged donkey.

I have based all these pieces on the scales, arpeggios and broken chords of the Grade One piano syllabus. It is very important to practise your scales and arpeggios as all the great composers use them in their pieces.

I wish you great success in your piano playing.

Malcolm Archer.

RED ROOSTER RAG

Scale of C major

DONKEY WITH A WOODEN LEG

Scale of C major

TRY TO CATCH AN ECHO

Scales of C and G major

MARCH

Scale of G major

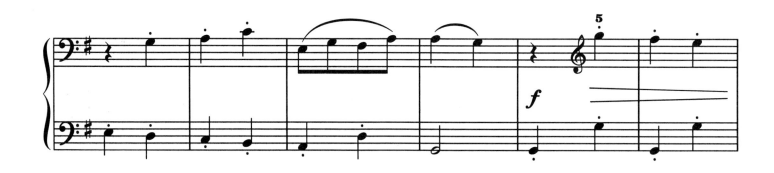

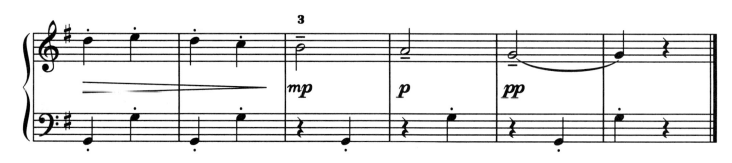

FOLLOW MY LEADER

Scale of G major

HIGHLAND DANCE

Scale of D major

SAILING

Scale of D major

GYMNOPODIE

Scale of F major

Andante cantabile ($\quad$ = 112)

LULLABY
Scale of F major

With gentle movement ($\quad$ = 100)

DON'T WAKE THE KITTEN

Scale of A minor

THE LONELY BEAR

Scale of A minor

A WALK IN THE WOOD

Scale of D minor

THE BOUNCY CASTLE

Scale of C major - contrary motion

THE WEARY WINDMILL

Arpeggios of C and G major

22

JAZZY FINGERS

Arpeggio of G major

THE WEDNESDAY WALTZ

Arpeggio of F major

A MOONLIGHT BREAKFAST

Arpeggios of A and D minor

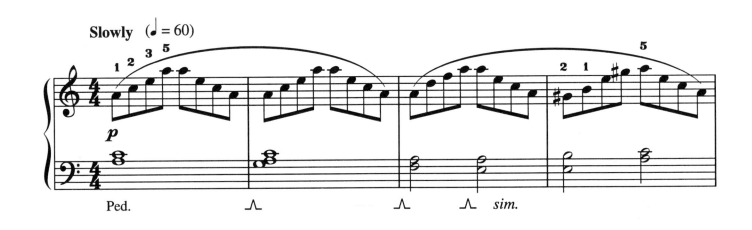

THE BANANA SKIN BALLET
Broken chord of G major

UP AND DOWN A RAINBOW

Broken chord of C major

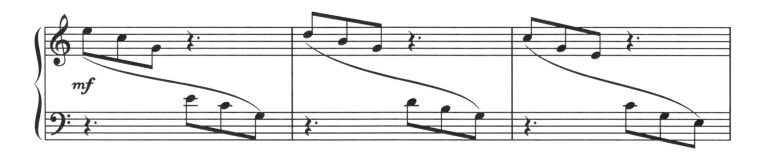

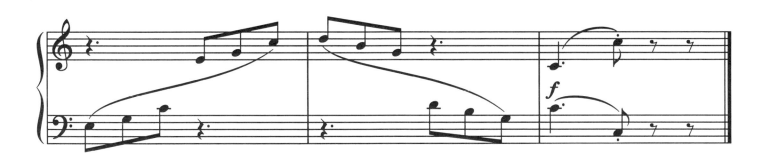

ASLEEP ON A CLOUD

Broken chords of C and F major

DREAMING
Broken chord of A minor

Poco adagio (♩ = 92)

LAMENT FOR A BROKEN CHORD

Broken chord of D minor